Cath Senker

WAYLAND

First published in 2014 by Wayland
Copyright © Wayland 2014

Wayland
338 Euston Road
London NW1 3BH

Wayland Australia
Level 17/207 Kent Street
Sydney, NSW 2000

Editor: Elizabeth Brent
Designer: Ray Bryant
Cover design by Rocket Design (East Anglia) Ltd.

Dewey number: 363.3'492-dc23

ISBN   978 0 7502 8101 0
eBook ISBN   978 0 7502 8548 3

Printed in China

10 9 8 7 6 5 4 3 2 1

Picture acknowledgements: All images, including cover image, courtesy of Shutterstock.com except: p8 © AFP/Getty Images; p11 © AFP/Getty Images (l), © STRINGER/Reuters/Corbis (r); p12 © ROB BLAKERS/epa/Corbis; p13 © Getty Images; p14 © Denver Post via Getty Images (t); p17 © Steven G. Smith/Corbis (r); p18 © ADREES LATIF/Reuters/Corbis; p19 © Denver Post via Getty Images; p20 © Juan Silva/Getty Images; p21 © AFP/Getty Images (l); p22 © AFP/Getty Images; p23 © EdStock/iStock Photo (l); p24 © HO/Reuters/Corbis; p26 © AFP/Getty Images.

Text acknowledgements: p11 Eyewitness: 'Witness describes Black Saturday fireballs', Callista Cooper, ABC News 24, 13 May 2009; p13 Case study: 'Rising from the Ashes', Claire Scobie, Edition 7, 2010 Future Living; p17 Eyewitness: Waldo Canyon Fire – Eye Witness Report Colorado Springs, Guerrilla Tag, 28 June 2012; p19 Case study: 'After Waldo Canyon', Fred Durso, Journal NFPA, 1 September 2012; p23 Eyewitness: 'Bolivia Requests International Aid to Fight Forest Fires', 19 August 2010, Bolivia Weekly; p25 Case study: 'Apoyo a la reactivacin productiva y elaboracin de estrategias para la gestin del riesgo y la prevencin de desastres a familias indgenas que han sido afectadas por lost incendios forestales del 2010, en el Beni-Bolivia', Marcelo Uwe Valdez Flores, 2011; p27 Quote: 'Fire Disturbance', Ivan Csiszar and Guido van der Werf, Food and Agriculture Organization (undated); p29 Quote: 'Fire and Smoke', NASA, 2013.

Wayland is a division of Hachette Children's Books, an Hachette UK company.
www.hachette.co.uk

Contents

What is a wildfire?

Have you ever seen an enormous bonfire? However large that seemed, a wildfire is much bigger! A wildfire is an uncontrolled fire in vegetation more than 1.8 m (almost 6 feet) high. It burns everything in its path – trees, homes, people and animals. Wildfires break out in various ways. Ground fires start on the forest floor, burning dried leaves and rotted wood. Here, there is little oxygen so fire spreads slowly, at about 3–5 km (2–3 miles) an hour, producing a lot of smoke. Surface fires burn grass, bushes and trees. Over open ground, they can travel at up to 23 km (14 miles) an hour – and even faster up slopes.

CROWN FIRES AND FIRESTORMS

Crown fires are the most dangerous, spread by the wind through the upper part of the trees. The flames leap from treetop to treetop. Crown fires use ladder fuels - shrubs, fallen trees and branches (they are called ladder fuels because they lead to fires higher up the trees). If strong air currents are drawn into the blaze, crown fires may turn into raging firestorms, burning even faster. With high winds, crown fires can move at up to 97 km (60 miles) per hour. The wind carries embers - glowing fragments of fire - which spark new wildfires elsewhere.

WORLD AT RISK

Dry areas such as the western USA often suffer wildfires. In southern France, powerful winds during the hot summer spread any fires in their path. Tropical forests, for example in South America, are at risk from accidental fires because people burn patches of forest for farming.

FACT BOX
The benefits of fire

Fires can be good for the environment. They kill off diseased trees and harmful insects and burn dead branches and grasses, returning nutrients to the soil. They blaze through the thick forest canopy and undergrowth, allowing sunlight to reach the forest floor so seedlings can grow. They help some types of trees to develop; fires help to open up some kinds of pine cones so they can start growing.

What causes wildfires?

Fires need three crucial ingredients: heat, oxygen and fuel – the 'fire triangle'. The heat to spark a wildfire can come from lightning, or electricity from power lines torn down in high winds. Oxygen is found in air. Branches, leaves and grass provide fuel. If one ingredient is missing, a burning fire will go out.

Human activity is a major cause of wildfires. In the USA, people cause 90 per cent of wildfires, often by throwing away lit cigarettes or leaving campfires burning. Some fires are started deliberately – this is called arson.

THE LINK TO CLIMATE CHANGE

Wildfires are a growing hazard because of climate change. Hotter, drier conditions are causing more droughts and stronger winds, which allow fires to spread more easily. Higher temperatures mean that winter snows occur later than usual. The snow melts earlier, so the land is drier for longer periods of time, increasing the risks. Alarmingly, the area that wildfires burn annually has doubled since 1960. Wildfires have also become a greater danger because an increasing number of homes are located in and around forests, creating more fuel for fires and putting lives at risk.

Firefighters trapped in a blazing forest can use fire shelters – aluminium tents that reflect heat. They have vents to allow firefighters to breathe but stop embers from entering.

This is the fire triangle, the three ingredients that are needed for a fire to burn.

Oxygen Heat Fire in proper balance Fuel

FACT BOX

Fighting wildfires

Firefighters often cannot reach wildfires in fire engines, so they fly over in helicopters or aeroplanes and dump water, foam or powder to douse the flames. Foams and powders have been developed that are better than water for putting out fire. Aircraft are also vital for observing the fire and transporting firefighters, supplies and equipment. Down on the ground, firefighters may beat the vegetation to smother the flames. They also use fire to fight fire — they burn or cut down a corridor of trees, which removes the fuel and creates a firebreak to stop the fire from spreading. Sometimes, specially trained firefighters called smokejumpers bravely parachute into isolated areas to fight fires, carrying equipment on their backs.

In February 2009, in the middle of the hot Australian summer, the country experienced a record heatwave. Temperatures soared up to a scorching 46.4° C (115.5° F) and fierce gale-force winds reached 90 km (56 miles) per hour. No rain fell for several weeks so the vegetation was tinder dry. Conditions were perfect for the deadly bushfires that erupted on 7 February – 'Black Saturday'.

In Victoria, south-east Australia, more than 47 major fires burst out, 14 of which caused damage or death. The worst was in Kilmore East, 90 km (56 miles) north of Melbourne, sparked by a faulty power pole. Flames leapt over the highway and set light to the forest, developing into a giant fireball. Steep slopes and strong winds allowed the fire to spread rapidly through several towns.

The fire spread so fast that it caught people unawares. Some tried to escape by car but were overwhelmed by the fire, which was so powerful it could kill with radiant heat (the heat you feel from a fire) from as far as 300 m (984 feet) away. The powerful wildfire rose 100 m (328 feet) above the tree line. It was so large that it appeared on NASA satellite images from space. Witnesses saw trees exploding and skies raining ash.

Bushfires can spread incredibly fast in high winds.

MORE TOWNSHIPS HIT

A change in the wind direction sends the fire north-east, where it strikes other settlements. At the same time, the Murrindindi fire hits the town of Marysville. Experts say that the two fires have released energy equal to 1,500 Hiroshima bombs – the nuclear bomb dropped on Japan in 1945 that killed 70,000 people instantly. Other parts of Victoria burn too, including Gippsland, in the east. In some places, the fire leaves few survivors. In Flowerdale, 65 km (40 miles) north of Melbourne, residents shelter in a pub for two days after their town is burnt down.

As bushfires rage, trees can explode into flames, posing a danger to firefighters.

Number of fires: more than 47

Wind speed: up to 90 kph (56 mph)

Number of homes destroyed: 2,100

Number of people killed: 173

Cost to economy: Aus $942 million (£564 million)

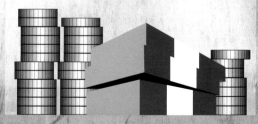

Disaster response

The Victoria fires caused the largest loss of life from bushfires in Australian history: 173 people lost their lives (120 of them in the Kinglake area) and 500 were injured. Of those who died, 113 people were found in or near homes that had burnt to the ground. Groups of bodies were discovered in cars. The flames had engulfed them while they attempted to flee. Property damage was extensive too; around 2,100 homes were destroyed. Large numbers of wild animals were killed and injured as their habitat burned.

TO THE RESCUE

More than 5,000 firefighters from all over Australia and New Zealand came to the rescue and other Australian states sent aid. Thousands of volunteers provided shelter and donations for the survivors. Many people were left with nothing. As one woman cried in despair, 'All I have left is what I stand up in and my bag. My house of 25 years is gone. I worked so hard to get that house!'

Prime Minister Kevin Rudd, understanding that 'some of these communities have nothing left', immediately offered emergency aid of Aus $10 million (£5.9 million).

'It went golden all around the house'

Peter Newman witnessed the fire from his home near Buxton, north-east of Melbourne. In the days before the fire, the temperature was rising and he knew wildfires were likely. His house was protected and had sprinklers so he and his wife stayed indoors, along with a friend and his daughter who had just lost their home to the fire. He recalled, 'It went golden all around the house . . . . From inside we could see out easily and watch the balls of flames hitting the deciduous trees around the house - where flames would go in and smoke would go out. We simply waited until balls of flames stopped going through the trees, because if you were in the way of those balls of flames, you were going to get fried just like the leaves were.' Fortunately, Mr Newman's group stayed safe as the fire swept over them.

This home has trees close to it and is likely to catch light. The residents have evacuated to a safe area.

Learning lessons

A Royal Commission report into the Black Saturday bushfires published in August 2009 criticized the emergency services' management of the firefighting operation. The County Fire Authority's warnings to communities in the path of the fire were inadequate. Many people did not realize the danger until the fire arrived. In July 2010, the final report recommended changes to the 'stay or go' policy. This policy suggests that people either stay in their home if it is protected against fire or leave as soon as they know a fire is approaching.

STAY

People defend their home and outbuildings with fire-resistant materials, for example, using asphalt rather than wooden shingles on the roof. They remove trees and bushes near buildings and cover attic vents with a wire screen so embers can't blow into the home. They have a hose and brooms ready to smother embers.

GO

People defend their home in the same way, but they evacuate after loading their car with food supplies, important documents and an emergency supply kit.

When bushfires occur, evacuation centres are set up to provide food and shelter.

Temporary housing was built for the residents of the Kinglake area who had lost their homes in the wildfire.

Case study

Kinglake rebuilds

The Kinglake area was devastated by the wildfires. As well as suffering the majority of the deaths, property losses included two schools, eight businesses and five shops. Some businesses lost up to 70 per cent of their customers. But the community pulled together to rebuild their lives. The Kinglake Business Hub was set up to provide office facilities to businesses that had lost their premises. One couple, Alan and Tricia Hayward, set up Tools for Tradies and Community Tool Libraries near Kinglake, to provide tools for tradespeople who had lost their equipment. As Kinglake resident Courtney Hall commented, 'it was an awakening - what life is about and what it's not. The blessings are the people I've met in the community on account of our tragedy.'

The western USA always experiences ideal wildfire conditions — drought, hot temperatures, high winds, thunderstorms and plenty of dry vegetation in forests and grasslands. But in 2012, the wildfires were more ferocious than usual. Serious fires broke out in several states, including New Mexico and California. Some of the worst fires were the High Park and Waldo Canyon fires in Colorado.

MASSIVE DESTRUCTION

On 9 June, lightning triggered the High Park fire. The second-largest fire Colorado had ever seen, it raged for three weeks and destroyed 259 homes. On 23 June, the Waldo Canyon fire broke out, just 6 km (4 miles) from Colorado Springs. Investigators later find out human action caused it. The fire presented a significant threat to homes, and 32,000 people were evacuated. By the time the wildfire was extinguished on 10 July, it had destroyed 7,384 hectares (18,246 acres) of forest and consumed around 347 homes. It was the most expensive fire in Colorado's history.

WHY WERE THE WILDFIRES SO HUGE?

Climate change has made the drought in the western USA more severe, the temperatures higher and the winds stronger. In 2012, the snow melted earlier, leaving the land dry for longer. The region has seen a growth in homes in or next to wildlands, drawn to the beautiful countryside and low crime rate. But the fire risks are huge. With greater numbers of people living in fire-prone regions, there are higher risks to life. Despite the below-average total number of fires in 2012 (55,505), the fires were bigger — the average size of a US fire was the highest on record.

The wild beauty of the Rocky Mountains of Colorado attracts new residents.

Some experts believe that fire-suppression policies have contributed to the problem. Firefighters have been successful at controlling small fires so the forests have become overgrown with dead branches and leaves. These build up and form excellent tinder for the big fires.

Number of fires:
4,167 (Colorado)

Wind speed:
up to 97 km (60 mph)

Number of homes destroyed:
606 (Waldo Canyon and High Park fires)

Number of people killed:
2 (Waldo Canyon); 1 (High Park)

Cost to economy:
US $538 million (£333 million) – Colorado

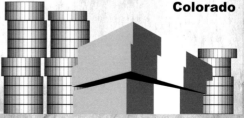

The Red Cross opened four shelters for evacuees from the Waldo Canyon fire, while a donation centre for the victims of the High Park Fire opened in Fort Collins, Colorado. Many people offered food for firefighters, shelter for neighbours or volunteered with the rescue effort. Members of the Volunteer Fire Departments battled the fires alongside professional firefighters.

COUNTING THE LOSSES

The Colorado wildfires were extinguished at great cost. Half of America's firefighting fleet were in Colorado, working 15-hour shifts in the fierce, exhausting heat. Overall, the Colorado fires destroyed 155,724 hectares (384,802 acres) of land and hundreds of homes. They caused record economic losses.

These homes were completely destroyed in the 2012 Waldo Canyon fire.

FAILURE TO PREPARE

The Colorado Springs Independent newspaper investigated the management of the Waldo Canyon fire. It found that the city was badly prepared even though wildfires had been raging nearby for three days. When the fire hit Mountain Shadows, only four firefighting vehicles were available. The evacuation plan had been drawn up only that morning, and was acted upon minutes before the first houses caught fire. Local firefighters did not have enough resources because the authorities failed to call for assistance until the fire had arrived. Firefighters did their best, but better planning could have reduced the losses.

Eyewitness

Waldo Canyon blazing

An eyewitness watched the scene. 'We're at the top of this hill . . . watching it all unfold. . . They've closed every exit going west. . . no one is allowed to go in. The fire-rescue crews are doing everything they can. They have also been able to send out several helicopters with 2 and 3,000-gallon (14,000-litre] snorkels [to fill with water while in flight]. They're flying out there, they're spotting new fires, small uprisings as fast as they can. . . . You can smell smoke in the air, you can see it, it's thick. Everyone's come together here. They're trying to get the animals out of their pens and barns as fast as they can and removing them to fairgrounds and shelters, even to people's homes. . . Hopefully we can get some rain . . . to help the firefighters.'

High winds fanned the flames of the Waldo Canyon wildfire.

Rebuilding communities

The wildfires left devastation in their wake. Homes, businesses and bridges had to be rebuilt, and electricity, water and gas lines repaired. Just one year later, some places had almost completed the reconstruction work. It proved easier to rebuild communities with homes built close together. People helped each other, for example, through community associations. However, people living in isolated homes with more land were less likely to return to the area because reconstruction was more costly.

WILDFIRE MITIGATION

After the Colorado wildfires, there was a big push to encourage communities to protect their properties from fire. The wildfire mitigation programme included putting in fire-resistant roofs; placing gravel around homes; removing trees and bushes near buildings; and covering attic vents with a wire screen so embers couldn't blow into the home. It was essential for neighbours to work together. If one person had a home that was not fire-safe, it would affect others' safety.

Case study

Despite the devastation, within a year, many homes were rebuilt.

Wildfire mitigation in Mountain Shadows

In Mountain Shadows, 392 homes were destroyed by the Waldo Canyon fire and two people died. Only five per cent of residents had taken part in wildfire mitigation efforts, and many homes had a high risk of catching fire. The Colorado Division of Fire Prevention and Control estimated that around a quarter of homes in Mountain Shadows had wooden roofs. In July 2012, Diane Paton returned to the site of her Mountain Shadows house to search for any belongings that had survived the blaze. Her grand piano was now a piece of charred wood and her car was a wreck. Diane managed to find a few documents and pieces of pottery. She was one of the few who had supported the mitigation efforts - she had gravel all around the house and no patches of trees nearby that could have caught fire. Just before the fire broke out, Diane had been thinking about replacing her wooden roof with a fire-resistant alternative - but she hadn't got round to it.

In Bolivia, South America, in August 2012, 25,000 wildfires raged in five of the country's nine regions. Fires covered 1.5 million hectares (3.7 million acres) of land – that's three-quarters of the size of Wales! Thick smoke blanketed the entire area. Worst hit were the rainforest lands in the Eastern and Amazon areas: Cochabamba, Beni, Santa Cruz, Pando and Tarija. Many small towns, villages and wildlife were in danger. Firefighters and local people worked in the burning fields, doing the best they could to stop the spread of the fire. But they had only buckets of water and branches of brush to stamp out the flames. They were fighting a losing battle. Some of the blazes were so powerful that firefighters could not approach them.

The fires were started by *chaqueos* – the deliberate burning of forests and grasslands in the summer to clear them to sow crops. This traditional practice of slash-and-burn agriculture was not harmful when it was on a small scale but when practised widely, it is easy for the fires to go out of control. Now *chaqueos* are illegal but it is hard to enforce the law. In 2010, insufficient rain and strong winds made it difficult to control the fires. Strong winds carried the smouldering embers through the air and they started new blazes.

RECORD HOTSPOTS

Climate change is the wider reason for the mounting hazards of wildfires. It is already affecting Bolivia. The temperature has been rising since the 1970s, causing more droughts, which lead to more frequent and more dangerous forest fires. Bolivia usually experiences major fires every two or three years, and each time, the damage is worse. A record 158,244 hotspots (active fire areas) erupted in 2010 – 40 per cent more than in 2009.

FACT BOX   Slash-and-burn agriculture

First, farmers burn down a small area of forest and clear it. The ash fertilizes the soil. Farmers plant their crops. After a few years, the soil becomes less fertile, so the farmers leave. The soil receives seeds and nutrients from the surrounding area, and plants grow back. The farmers shift to a new plot and start again. Nowadays, so much land is cleared that large areas remain deforested and do not grow back.

Impact and response

The forest fires caused immense destruction; people lost their homes, land and livelihood as their crops burnt. Forests and wildlife were destroyed in national parks in Santa Cruz, Pando and Beni. As the forests burned, harmful gases were released into the atmosphere, contributing to global warming.

FEW FIREFIGHTING RESOURCES

As in many poor countries, the Bolivian government did not have the resources to battle large-scale wildfires. It had no water-bombing aircraft to reach the forest blazes. Firefighters used just basic equipment — a machete to cut through trees, a *matafuegos* (rubber stick for beating flames) and water to put out fire in their path.

President Evo Morales admitted the government could not fight the wildfires effectively but blamed the people who were burning the vegetation, saying that those who set a fire should make sure they have cleared the area so the fire does not leap across to other areas.

NEIGHBOURS STEP IN

The government was forced to buy firefighting equipment in a hurry, and the President asked for help from neighbouring countries. Chile, Argentina and Brazil sent firefighters, equipment and experts. Yet the fires continued for several months, only ending with the winter rains.

Eyewitness

A total disaster

Weimar Becerra, the director-general of Forest Management and Development reported that the wildfire was most dangerous in the Amazon region of Pando, the Puerto Rico municipality and the Manuripi Wildlife Reserve. He asked for international assistance to extinguish this fire, which threatened to destroy this area of great biodiversity and cause an environmental disaster. He declared, 'We have six forest fires exceeding 50 metres (164 feet) in height which are growing and we don't have the national resources to extinguish them. The fires have been destroying nearly everything in their path and the ash fall has been contaminating rivers and killing fish.'
19 August 2010

Prevention, protection and education

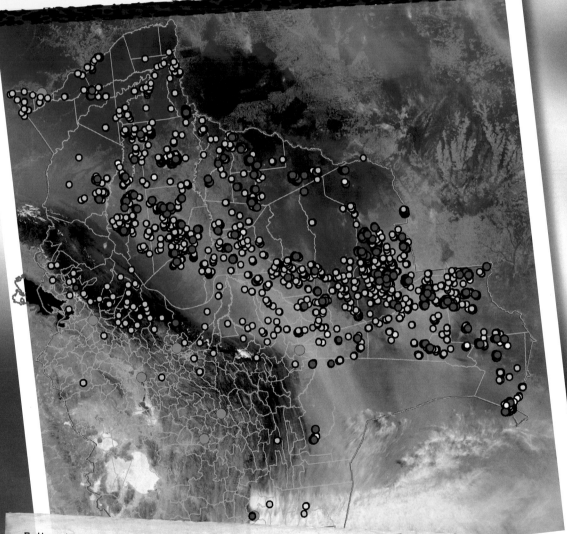

Following the fires, in 2011, the government adopted a plan for the 'prevention, monitoring and combat' of forest fires. It aimed to reduce forest loss and the emission (giving off) of gases from burning trees into the atmosphere, which contributes to global warming. The government invested US $28 million (£17 million) in firefighting teams, helicopters for monitoring fires, and training the armed forces in firefighting. It made agreements with farmers in the region to try to prevent fires, and promoted alternative practices to avoid clearing land by burning, protect the environment and improve living conditions in rural areas. The authorities would carry out inspections in the area and use satellite images to keep an eye on the situation. Those caught setting uncontrolled fires would pay fines.

NOT ENOUGH

However, more efforts are needed to protect the forests from deforestation. Detection needs to be improved; only half of fires are revealed by satellite because many occur at ground level and are hidden by vegetation. Stricter controls over the illegal use of fire to clear land are also necessary. Large companies still carry out the practice. If they are caught, they simply pay a fine and carry on. It might help to reward firms that avoid damaging the forest, for example, by paying higher prices for their products.

Case study

Bolivian farmers planting garlic close to the forest.

Protecting the forest, improving lives

In 2011, indigenous people in the Mojos province, who had been affected by the 2010 fire, took part in a programme run by charities to educate them about the risks of wildfires and help them to adapt to climate change by returning to growing traditional crops in the forest. Local people gained awareness of the hazards of using fire and how to reduce them. They discovered how to protect the woods by creating firebreaks in the forests and constructing wells to provide water to put out fires. The participants learnt traditional farming methods, including keeping seeds from their crops to save the cost of buying new seeds each year. They found that growing their own food raised their living standards as well as protecting the forest.

Prediction and prevention

Experts track bushfires at an operations centre in Sydney, Australia.

Unlike other natural disasters such as tsunamis and super storms, wildfires can often be prevented. People can be educated through classes, workshops or online resources to reduce the accidental setting of fires.

PREDICTION: FORECASTING AND MONITORING

The likelihood and the path of wildfires can be predicted using accurate weather forecasting and monitoring through remote sensing (scanning the Earth from a satellite) to check the temperature, humidity and wind. Mapping of wildfire trends is useful. For example, a map has been created that plots US wildfires between 2001 and 2012, showing where they erupted and their intensity. Long-term fire monitoring is important because climate change is rapidly altering the situation. It allows researchers to predict which areas need to be managed better to prevent the spread of fires.

Although these hi-tech methods exist, in the USA, old-fashioned look-out posts remain the main fire-detection method. An individual scans the landscape, often using a fire finder, a device with a round map on a table for working out the location of a fire. Some look-out posts have TV cameras to scan the landscape. The posts are manned all summer, especially in the western USA. When a person spots smoke, he or she contacts a dispatcher, giving the location, colour and shape of the smoke, its direction and the speed at which it is travelling. White smoke indicates a grass fire, while dark blue or black smoke usually means trees are on fire. Then the dispatcher contacts the firefighters.

DETECTION: SATELLITES AND SENSORS

Scientists are continually working on satellite technology to improve fire detection. Today's satellites have infrared sensors to detect heat, and light sensors to record smoke and other signs of fire. NASA's unmanned aircraft Ikhana can photograph fires through the smoke with special sensors, and the data is passed on to firefighters.

Expert view

Monitoring fires is essential

'Information on fire activity is used for global change research, estimating atmospheric emissions and developing periodic global and regional assessments, and for planning and operational purposes . . . and development of informed policies.' Ivan Csiszar and Guido van der Werf, Food and Agriculture Organization

Protection from wildfires

PRESCRIBED BURNING

Prescribed burning is used to protect communities from uncontrolled wildfires. It is the deliberate burning of shrubs, vegetation and trees in areas at risk of fire, to reduce the fuel available. Some experts believe that prescribed burning reduces catastrophic wildfires, although others argue that it does not greatly reduce their severity. Another method is creating firebreaks to stop wildfires spreading (see page 7).

FIRE-RESISTANT HOMES

Views on the 'stay or go' strategy (see page 12) have changed. The advice now is to leave immediately if there's a fire warning. However, in the USA, a few 'Shelter in place' communities, for example, the Rancho Santa Fe Fire Protection District in California, have been designed with the latest technology. The homes are located away from slopes, use top-quality fire-resistant materials and have sprinklers. All trees, bushes and grass near the houses are trimmed back. If fire threatens, people are urged to stay in their homes but not to fight the fire.

Few people can afford homes like this but they can adopt measures to protect their houses. The greatest risk to homes is from embers. People may think the danger is over, but days later, embers can start a new fire. They can adapt their homes with fire-resistant materials to prevent this from happening (see page 12) and spray houses with non-toxic foam to protect them from flames.

Expert view

A future of fierce fires

'Wildfires follow a simple but dangerous equation: Hotter, dryer conditions + more people in the world = a greater likelihood that there will be more ferocious wildfires threatening lives and property. As temperatures around the world rise, even areas not accustomed to seeing wildfires could be at risk in the future.'
NASA, 2013

LOOKING TO THE FUTURE

Community protection schemes are urgently needed as climate change increases the likelihood of severe wildfires in the future. Areas that already suffer wildfires are likely to see more, and new regions could be at risk. Reducing the hazards to people, property and wildlife is a key issue for communities worldwide.

Glossary

air current   The movement of air in a particular direction.

asphalt   A thick, black, sticky substance used for making the surface of roads.

atmosphere   The mixture of gases that surrounds the Earth.

bush   In Australia, a large, uncleared area, usually forested.

bushfire   A fire in a large area of rough open ground, especially one that spreads quickly.

canopy   A layer of tree branches over the top of a forest.

climate change   Changes in the Earth's temperature, wind patterns and rainfall, especially the increase in the temperature of the atmosphere that is caused by the increase of particular gases, especially carbon dioxide.

deciduous   The type of trees that lose their leaves in the autumn.

deforested   When all the trees in a place have been cut down and destroyed.

drought   A long period of time when there is little or no rain.

ember   A piece of wood or coal that is still red and hot after a fire has died, and can start a new fire.

evacuate   To move people from a place of danger to a safer place.

fertilize   To add a substance to soil to make plants grow more successfully.

fireball   A bright ball of fire.

firebreak   Something that stops a fire from spreading, such as a strip of land in a forest that has been cleared of trees.

fire-resistant   Something that has been treated so that it will not catch fire easily.

forecasting   Making a statement about what will happen in the future, based on information that we have now.

global warming   The rise in temperature of the Earth's atmosphere that is caused by the increase of particular gases, especially carbon dioxide.

habitat   The place where a particular type of animal or plant is normally found.

heatwave   A period of unusually hot weather.

humidity   The amount of water in the air.

indigenous   Belonging to a particular place rather than coming to it from somewhere else.

infrared   Rays like light but lying outside the visible spectrum (light you can see) at its red end.

intensity   Being intense – very great or very strong.

look-out post   A place where you look out for a particular danger.

mitigation   Making something less of a problem.

monitor   To watch and check something over a period of time in order to see how it changes.

nutrient   A substance that is needed to keep a living thing alive and to help it to grow.

prediction   A statement that says what you think will happen.

reconstruction   Rebuilding something that has been damaged or destroyed.

Royal Commission   A group of people that a government chooses to look into a particular law or subject and suggest any changes or new laws that should be introduced.

satellite   An electronic device that is sent into space and moves around the Earth or another planet. It is used for communicating, for example by radio or television, and for providing information.

sensor   A device that can react, for example to light or heat, in order to show something.

slash-and-burn agriculture   A kind of farming in which trees and plants are cut down or burnt so that crops can be sown.

smokejumper   A special firefighter who parachutes down to the scene of a fire with equipment to fight it.

tinder   Dry material, especially wood or grass, that burns easily and can become fuel for a fire.

tropical   Relating to the tropics, the area just above and below the Equator. The climate is warm or hot, and moist all year round.

vegetation   Plants in general, especially the plants that are found in a particular area or environment.

vent   An opening that allows air, gas or liquid to pass out of or into a room or building.

wildland   Areas that are wild and little changed by humans.

Find out more

Books
Non-fiction
Disaster Watch: Wildfires by Paul Mason (Smart Apple Media, 2012)

Earth in Action: Wildfires by Rebecca Rowell (Core Library, 2013)

Natural Disasters: Wildfires by Rochelle Baltzer (Big Buddy Books, 2011)

Real World Math: Natural Disasters: Wildfires by Tamra B. Orr (Cherry Lake Publishing, 2012)

Smoke Jumper by Nick Gordon (Torque, 2012)

The Worst Wildfires Of All Time by Suzanne Garbe (Capstone Press, 2012)

Fiction
Dark Water (Audio CD) by Laura McNeal (Brilliance Audio, 2011)

Wildfire: Code Red by Chris Ryan (Red Fox, 2007)

Wildfire Run by Dee Garretson (HarperCollins, 2011)

Websites
Black Saturday Bushfires
http://www.blacksaturdaybushfires.com.au
Information, map and photos about the bushfires

Colorado Wildfires 2012
http://www.huffingtonpost.com/2012/06/25/colorado-wildfires-2012-v_n_1623695.html#slide=1163280
About the wildfires, with photographs

Fire and Smoke
http://www.nasa.gov/mission_pages/fires/main/index.html#.UmeTlxae6e9
NASA site with details of current wildfires around the world and technology to track wildfires

How Wildfires Work
http://science.howstuffworks.com/nature/natural-disasters/wildfire.htm
How wildfires occur, with links to prevention and smokejumpers

Only YOU can prevent wildfires
http://www.smokeybear.com/wildfires.asp
US site about wildfire science, preventing and fighting wildfires

Wildfires
http://www.weatherwizkids.com/weather-wildfire.htm
US site about wildfires with safety tips

Films
Bolivian wildfires 2010
http://www.dailymotion.com/video/xfrhyl_bolivian-fires-turn-catastrophic_newsc
Footage of the fires

Wildfires – National Geographic
http://video.nationalgeographic.com/video/player/environment/environment-natural-disasters/wildfires-env
Videos of wildfires, smokejumpers and creating firebreaks to reduce wildfires

Index

PLANET IN PERIL

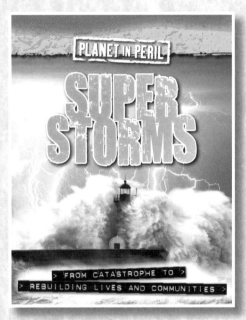

978-0-7502-8299-4

978-0-7502-8102-7

978-0-7502-8100-3

978-0-7502-8101-0

WAYLAND